Perspectives of a Butterfly

by Leah Nicole

PO Box 9523
Hampton, Virginia 23670
1(757) 825-0030
ItsmeDrIFP.org

© *2015 Leah Nicole. All Rights Reserved*

No part of this book may be reproduced, stored in a retrieval system, or transmitted by any means without the written permission of the author.

First published by dpRochelle 10/28/15

ISBN: 978-0-9862389-6-3

Printed in the United States of America
Hampton, Virginia

Reference

All biblical scriptures are quoted from the King James Version unless otherwise noted.

Acknowledgements

I would like to give special thanks to my mom, Renee Williams, for all of her love and support throughout my life, and to Jeremiah and Silas, mommy's little soldiers, who fill my heart with joy and laughter.

Thanks to:

Dr. I. Franklin Perkins
Pastor Derrick Perkins, Sr.
Aegious S. Perkins

Contents

Chapter 1
    Rejection   7

Chapter 2
    Accepting God's Grace   15

Chapter 3
    Sweeping Out the Cobwebs   23

Chapter 4
    Transformation   29

Chapter 5
    Watch Out for the Wolves   37

Chapter 6
    Defeating the Fear   45

Chapter 7
    Just a Time of Thanks   53

Perspectives of a Butterfly

Introduction

As a child, one may wonder how their life will turn out. Well at least I did. I know how I wanted my life to be and the paths I had planned for myself. However, one thing I have come to learn in life is that most times things do not go according to "our" plan. There are twists, turns, bumps, road blocks and so many other surprises for which we do not plan. Even our plan B's and plan C's do not always work out. In any case, life has a way of telling its own story even though we are the ones writing the book. If we could predict our future, would there really be a point for day to day life?

I used to ask myself, "What is life going to bring my way today?" In some instances, this is a valid question. However, depending on your state of mind and emotions that day, it could be a very disheartening question. You see, there is power in the tongue. The words you choose can build and repair or damage and destroy. Therefore, it is important to be aware of how you address or talk about things because it can have an effect on your outlook, as well as, the outlook of others. Perhaps it may cause you to expect the worst. So, I then began rephrasing the question by asking, "What will I bring to life today?"

You see, at any moment, life can "hit" you like a train. Whether it is the death of a loved one, a broken relationship, a family feud, or illness, life brings unexpected circumstances and situations. Then there are times when we actually bring them on ourselves. Whatever the case, asking the first question of "What is life going to bring my way today," leads me to feel like I was getting run over by this train constantly. However, when I rephrase it, I find myself coming at life like a train . . . on the move and ready to push through whatever comes my way. I find myself not getting run over anymore, but just damaged a bit and off track sometimes. Nevertheless, it is easier for me to bounce back.

Anyway, my goal for this book is to help you look at life with a different perspective so you would not feel like you are always tied to the train track. There are different ways to approach, challenge, understand, and survive the "hits" of life. Hopefully, in reading this, you will learn other ways to cope or deal with situations that comes your way. If not, then at least enjoy some of the poetry from my heart.

No one knows what their journey entails.

Perhaps it is full of wonder and gain.

For some it may have more roads filled with pain.

No matter the journey, whether rough or ease,

Never forget to fall on your knees.

For it is in our falling, that we see a different view.

By not focusing on the obstacles but on the One who will carry you through.

Chapter 1
Rejection

Who likes rejection? Just the word itself has a tendency to make people cringe. It is one I know all too well. It is a painful feeling. From an absentee father, to school bullies, from a high school recluse, to broken relationships, rejection has always been a part of my life. If everyone is honest with themselves, then all can say . . . we know what it feels like to be rejected in some way, shape, or form. We may have even been the person to reject someone else. It is a horrible feeling that tries to kill our spirit and steal our joy. We are made to feel as though we are not good enough, that we do not measure up, that there is something faulty within us that cause others to turn us away. And then what do we do? We question ourselves. "What's wrong with me?" "Where did I go wrong?" "What do I need to change about myself?"

If I could go back and talk to my childhood self, I would answer these questions with, "Nothing is wrong with me, I am beautiful, in spite of . . ." If there is anything to change, I would say it would be the attitude in which I take rejection.

We cannot let how others treat us be our basis for how we judge and see ourselves. By doing this, we then let low self-esteem, depression, and other issues overwhelm our lives. We must remember that we are "fearfully and wonderfully made." (Psalms 139:14)

I am reminded of One who was rejected even by those closest to Him. Yes, Jesus faced rejection that far surpassed any other. Thinking on this lets me know that I have the same strength to stand in the face of rejection simply because I am His. I understand that sometimes I will be rejected because I stand up or stand out for what is right. Or perhaps it is just not the direction in which God wants me to go. This causes rejection to force me towards my destiny. Sure it hurts, and it is not comfortable, but sometimes it is a necessary evil to propel me to a greater purpose. If they did not reject Christ Jesus, would He have been nailed to the cross for our sins? Then where would we be? Think about it.

Instead of seeing it as rejection, consider it redirection. Redirect your thoughts and feelings to consider where God is taking you. Seek Him for consolation, as well as, instruction. Remember, He received more rejection than any of us . . . and still does. However, it was all for a reason. We just have to trust and believe that God knows best. *"Trust in the Lord with all thine heart; and lean not unto thine own understanding."* (Proverbs 3:5)

Grow From It

Sometimes people can ruin a moment for you.
It's up to you on how long that moment lasts.
Life's joy should not be based upon temporary emotions,
nor upon time of the past.

Sometimes the wind blows just to get the dust out of your eye.
Sometimes the rain falls just to get you clean.
Sometimes the storms come just to ruffle your feathers.
Sometimes the rainbow takes longer to be seen.

Yet, it all helps you to grow.
It all helps you to learn.
The Hebrew boys were in the fire,
but God didn't let them burn.

Many times praise is the main ingredient to get you through;
refreshing your spirit like morning dew.

Baby, To Be Honest

I could tell you that this world is gonna love you,
that you'll never have a worry or care.
But that wouldn't be telling the truth
And I can't send you out unaware.

There's a lot of mean people, baby.
They may try to hurt you and break you down.
But you can't let them break your spirit,
and when it comes to being yourself, stand your ground.

I could tell you that life is a box of chocolate,
and you never know what will be inside.
But the truth is it's not all sweet,
and sometimes you may want to run and hide.

But you can't let fear stop you from living.
You have a destiny that you must fulfill.
The roads you take won't always be easy,
sometimes you'll walk in a valley, and sometimes you'll climb a hill.

But take courage my dear sweet baby,
for you don't have to go through this alone.
No, mama can't always go with you,
but there is One who sits on the throne.

I pray that He guides you daily,
so I teach you now to stay in His Word and pray.
When you feel like you need direction,
He will be there to show you the way.

When you're at your lowest moment
and you feel there is no one who cares.
I pray that His Spirit comforts you,
for the Lord's grace and mercy will always be right there.

Chapter 2
Accepting God's Grace

Have you ever had that moment when you felt that you did something so bad that you could not tell anyone about it? Not even God?! I have . . . several times. I have made numerous mistakes in this adult life of which I am not proud. Some I even cringe at the memory and wish I could just erase it away. Yeah, that bad . . .

Of course, it is at this time that the enemy tries to get in your head and say, "You've screwed up big time! How can you even think about talking to God after this? He is not going to hear a word you say!" I do not know about you, but I have fallen into the trap of believing these lies a few times. I even had in my mindset that I would give God a few days to cool off from being mad at me, and then I would go to Him and ask His forgiveness. I am so glad He did not let me leave this earth before I got to ask for that forgiveness!

It was not until I had children that I realized how ridiculous that logic was. When my kids break something or do something they are not supposed to do, I have taught them to tell me immediately and not try to hide it. Telling me immediately leads me to be a bit more lenient with them, as opposed to them hiding it or telling me days later. It also helps me to trust them more, and at the same time, they learn to trust that it is ok to tell mommy when things go wrong. I appreciate their honesty and the fact that they feel comfortable enough to know that they can come to me about anything. God is the same way. First off, He knows all and sees all. To think that we can hide anything from Him is absurd. Secondly, He is our Father who loves us beyond measure and beyond compare. He loves us through and past our faults. He wants us to come to Him for everything . . . good and bad. Thirdly, this is why He sent His Son Jesus. He knew that we would mess up sometimes, so Jesus paid that price for us years ago. So, He is always right there waiting for us, with open arms, to just say "Father, I messed up. Sorry. I will try to do better next time." Hey, if a child can do it, then an adult can do it also. Once we do that, INSTANTLY, we are forgiven. There is no waiting period. The waiting period was completed those three days after Jesus died on the cross. Therefore, we can run to Him and pour out our heart, our tears, and our faults without the fear of Him turning us away. We have to learn to fall *into* His grace, even if we feel like we have fallen out. His grace is sufficient. *"My grace is sufficient for thee: for my strength is made perfect in weakness . . ."* (II Corinthians 12:9)

Saved By Grace

My soul is lying in wait . . .
while life passes me by.
Work rush . . . school rush . . .
No time to meditate . . . I'm running late for rehearsal . . .
running late for a meeting.
It can wait til late . . . til tomorrow.
No thoughts of future sorrow.
I gotta go . . . don't got time . . . I'm . . .

Lying in wait . . .
while blessings pour my way.
A place of my own . . . thank you . . .
A new ride . . . thank you . . .
A check in the mail . . . thank you . . .
is all I have time for at the moment.
No time for atonement.
Just a simple thanks for each thing,
but it's not quantity, it's quality you desire.
A soul that's on fire . . . willing to strive and never tire.

And then . . . the alarm goes off . . .
my spirit rises anew,
ending my procrastination
and your frustration of something long overdue.
So I walk towards my destination . . .
my place . . .
my concrete foundation on which I must base

my every step . . . my daily plan.
Trying not to waste
a second of time,
a moment of truth,
a cent of a dime,
a day of youth.

Having speculations of obliteration, frustration and fabrications.
Yet, love diluting hate
And peace diluting fear
Bring about concentration on true edification.
Denial of myself . . .
Rejection of that which isn't mine . . .
Unblinded by fame and wealth . . .
Embracing not my will, but Thine.
Accepting in my heart the Light that shines.

In Spite of Me

The Spirit's killing my flesh with convictions
of my life's contradictions.
Just going to sleep causes frictions.
For fear it seems I just want to run.
Is not Christ Jesus the One to soothe my heart when I'm lonely?
Give me bread when I'm hungry?
Comfort me when I'm scared?

Yes, His right hand will uphold me,
but this world's driving me crazy.
Through my eyes life is hazy.
Am I coming or going?
Which road do I take?
Although I try to do right I end up making mistakes
and demons laugh in my face.
It's time I retaliate,
but my knowledge is limited.
I get my smarts from these streets.
I can't do it alone, Lord . . . I'm feeling so weak.

In my silence and tears I feel you remove my fears . . .
blanketing me with Your love,
tucking me in Your peace,
and lulling my soul to assurance saying . . .
"Fear not, for I am with you.

With all your heart trust in Me and I'll lead you.
Your faith comes by hearing and not by sight.
So study My Word both day and night."

And when it feels I might fall,
Jesus, it's Your name I call
'cause You're the One that can save . . .
The only One that can raise me from this pit I've fallen in.
You can wash away all my sin,
And I know I'll be born again 'cause Your love is amazing!

From my chains of circumstance, Your love liberates me.
Devil's upset 'cause his plans failed to incinerate me.
Like a bolt of lightning, Your power it generates me.
It starts me witnessing to those who are considering
taking a chance on my Savior.
The One and only Creator.
Above You there is none greater.

Chapter 3
Sweeping the Cobwebs

After I accept God's forgiving grace for whatever I did wrong, I then had to learn to sweep out the cobwebs. By this, I mean forgetting the guilt of the wrong doing and moving on with my life. I am not a fan of spiders. They are my number one bug enemy. The worst part is walking into their webs. They are sticky and they catch things like all kinds of other bugs and dust.

I like to think of the guilt of our wrongs as cobwebs. Every time we dwell on it, we are throwing dust on it. Every time we let someone bring it up and bring us down, is another bug or piece of dust it has caught. Yet, the spider (or wrong) is long gone and over. So why keep the cobweb around? There is no use for it, and it is not a pretty sight. So clean it up and let it go.

No, we may not forget where it was, in other words the wrong may never leave our memory. However, that is what helps to be a reminder to not let it reoccur. The point I am trying to make is that we should not dwell on the mistake, but learn from it, remembering to avoid it in the future. When the memory comes back or someone tries to throw it in our faces or hold it over our heads, there will be nothing to catch and hold that negativity, so the memory has no choice but to fall away.

The loving sacrifice of Jesus paved the way for us to stand blameless before the Lord. It is because of His death and resurrection that we are reconciled to God. This is why it is so important to accept Him as our Lord and Savior. Now, when God looks at us, He does not see all our sin and wrong, but He sees the blood of His Son, Jesus, covering us. Therefore, once we ask to be forgiven, we should understand that God has thrown our sins into the depths of the sea, never to resurface. So, if He does not bring our sins back up, then why should we? And why should we allow others to remind us? *". . . I will put my laws into their hearts, and in their minds will I write them; And their sins and iniquities will I remember no more."*
(Hebrews 10:16-17)

Help

Rescue me from myself.
Free me from my mind.
Release the burdens in my soul.
Break these chains of fear that bind.

Cleanse my thought of negativity.
Wash the worry from my heart.
Wipe away the tears that drown me.
Help me forth to a new start.

I have come to know much sorrow.
I have come to feel great pain.
I have come to hear the bellow of frustration.
Depressing clouds have brought much rain.

Shredded memories trash my mind;
Regrets I fear and dare not tell.
On an endless sea of desolation,
living life's become a living hell.

Help me please to free my spirit.
My heart's a dusty, cobwebbed shelf.
Shed some light that I might rise,
for I cannot save myself.

Masked

Hidden in my laugh,
a cry of utter pain.
Enveloped by my eyes,
are tears to cause a rain.

Clouded by my future,
memories storm my mind.
Shadowed by my smile,
my words are hard to find.

But away with this masquerade.
Come forth my every groan.
No more of the deafening silence.
I know I'm not here alone.

Scream out my courageous heart.
Bellow loud my oppressed soul.
No more hiding my true feelings.
Time for me to take control.

No longer letting shame consume me.
Won't let their whispers prick my spirit.
Free from the broken chains of my past.
My future gets brighter as I learn not to fear it.

Chapter 4
Transformation

Maybe you are reading this book right now and you are saying to yourself, "Grace is all fine and good, but what if I have not accepted Jesus yet?" Perhaps you think you have to get your life together first. Perhaps you have not given it much thought. Whatever the reason may be, it is important for you to know that there is no better time than right now.

When I was a kid in elementary school, we had a caterpillar for our class pet. It was awesome to see him crawl around and eat the leaves. (Yes, there are some bugs that I do like). Anyway, eventually the caterpillar stopped growing and began to form this shell around it making it a pupa. That pupa sat there for a few weeks. We all wondered what was happening in that tiny shell. We could not see, but we knew it was something wondrous. Then one day, a few weeks later, out of that small shell began to emerge a beautiful colorful butterfly. So not only did this tiny creature change into something beautiful, but it could fly.

When we welcome Jesus into our lives, we are just like that caterpillar. We have eaten all this world has to offer, yet nothing changes. Then we stop and realize we are covered (encased) by sin and shame. We then give Jesus control to take over and change us from the inside. He touches the innermost part of us that no one else can touch or change. Though others may not see it right away, we know that he is in there working on our hearts. Eventually, over time the change is seen by others and they are able to see His wondrous works. Once we emerge, we are free from the bondage of sin and shame. We can then fly to new heights in Him.

Waiting for your life or situation to change, or even your mind to change will not only be a waste of time, but possibly the biggest mistake of your life. You see, if we could change ourselves and circumstances, then there would have been no need for Jesus to sacrifice His life. He tells us to come as we are. He came for the sinner, not the perfect. He came for the broken, and we are all broken in some way. That means come with your guilt, your fears, your frustrations, and your pain. Whatever it is, He can handle it. He is the only One who can.

Let us think about it. If you could fix it, you would have fixed it by now. We often try to fix things backwards by starting from the outside. We try to work harder, eat better, dress nicer, smile more, etc. But all of these things are temporal. God works on the inside by changing our hearts and renewing our minds because our soul is eternal. Once we allow Him to work on the inside, our whole point of view will change regarding the outside and our circumstances. Our worries will not weigh and burden us as before because we learn to continually cast our cares upon Him since He's the only One knows what to do about them. He gives us a peace that no man can give, even in our darkest moments.

This is not to say that once you accept Jesus everything will always be well with you, or all of your days will be bright and sunny. It simply means that you will be able to get through things better because your Daddy has your back. Even more so, you have the hope in knowing that when this life is over, you will have an eternity with Him free of all pain and sorrow of this world. And that is something to look forward to for sure! *"For God so loved the world that He gave His only begotten Son, that whosoever believeth in Him should not perish, but have everlasting life."* (John 3:16)

Sinner's Testimony

I was sitting there all alone,
a heart without a home;
no one to care for me,
no one was there for me,
No friend to call my own.

So, Lord, I came to You.
I hoped You would come through.
You said to just pray,
and to ask in a way,
and all the rest You would do.

Lord, please hear me as I call on Your name.
Oh, Lord, I'm not asking for fortune or fame,
but Lord, I'm asking if this one thing You'll do,
guide my heart, Jesus, and help me get through.

Lord, I remember when . . .
My life was full of sin,
but You came into my life.
Lord, You showed me the light.
Now I am born again.

I walk that road no more.
It's You who I adore.
You lifted me up.

Lord, You filled up my cup.
I will live with You forever more.

Lord, please hear me as I call on Your name.
Oh, Lord, I'm not asking for fortune or fame,
but Lord, I'm asking if this one thing You'll do,
guide my heart, Jesus, and help me get through.

Testimony

He tried to destroy me from the time I was in my mother's womb.
My life and soul he wanted to consume.
Even as a child he put dreams in my head,
and evil figures with noises in my room.

Then I became a teen so he rolled different paths my way,
each one leading to doom . . .
Drugs . . . sex . . . rebellion . . . gangs . . .
Whispering in my ear "Go ahead, do ya thang."

But I stayed on the right path still.
Then I guess he got upset,
'cause when I got older he pulled out the big guns for real.
You know, the time when I was given wings.
But it was with the wrong flock I began to fly.
There I was sinking deeper and deeper,
though, I thought I was on a high
but grace and mercy saved me time after time . . .
snare after snare.

I was oblivious to the fact that You were even there.
I was laying down my life, but not for what was right.
As sin was taking control almost every other night.
Blessed I was the one You chose not to smite,
but You opened my eyes and gave me my sight.

Sight to see the life I was livin'
was not the reason my life was given.
Sight to see I had to stop sinnin'
finally started stomping on his head and started winnin'.

So I cried to You in darkness, swallowed by sin and shame,
calling on Your name,
praying You'd save a wretch like me.
A person who had eyes and did not want to see.
A person who had ears but ignored the calling.
A person who had foundation but steadily kept falling.
A person who was gifted but wouldn't receive Your presence.

Realizing I had made my own self a peasant . . .
my own self sin's slave.
With every act of sin I was digging my own grave.
Ahhh . . . but You being You,
the One and Only who could pull me through.
Even when in my heart I wasn't sure I would stay true.
You being the loving God You are.
You being the Almighty Lord You are.
You being the forgiving Father You are.
You being the only One who could bring me this far.
Lost for words, I wave my hand . . .
and just thank and praise You.

Chapter 5
Watch Out for the Wolves

Now understand that when you give your life to Christ, the devil gets extremely angry. It not only means that he has lost another soul, but also that there is another soldier in God's army that will be spreading the Gospel of Jesus Christ. In other words, gear up . . . you are going into battle. Satan will try to distract, discourage, and destroy you. However, I like to remember the scripture that states *"Greater is He that is in me, than he that is in the world."* (1 John 4:4) As long as we stand on the Word of God and keep our trust in Him, we will not be defeated.

So, everyone knows the story of Little Red Riding Hood. If not . . . look it up. You know the part where she sees grandma in the bed and notices her big ears, big eyes, and big teeth? She had all these red flags (no pun intended) giving her a sign that it was not her grandmother. However, she stayed right beside grandma believing it was her. Perhaps it was curiosity or maybe even ignorance. Whatever the case may be, the fact of the matter is that she ignored the red flags. Hence, she got eaten alive.

I have been Little Red a few times in my life. Normally, my reasoning was, I wanted to see the good in people. So, I often ignored the signs and clues. I have ignored the voice of the Holy Spirit telling me that the intentions of a person were not good. I have been eaten alive mentally and emotionally by these wolves. It got me a bunch of tears and in a bunch of messes. It is important to remember that everyone who says they are for you may not be for you, but have hidden agendas. Sometimes their motives are to hurt you and other times they choose to use you to get what they want. Often times the wolves come in disguise to attack your area of weakness, whether it is men, women, quick money, or the need for attention. If you know you are at your weakest moment, watch out . . . there is a wolf somewhere around. The enemy knows what our weaknesses are, so he has snares designed to trap us. God's Word says that we must be aware of the enemy's devices.

In being the victim so many times, I have learned to watch out for the not so inconspicuous actions. Most importantly, I pray daily to be more in tune with God's Holy

Spirit in order to discern the difference. Yes, we are supposed to help others, and use wisdom to spend our resources, time, and emotions wisely and on the right people or things. Do not let the wolves steal what belongs to you. Pay attention to the signs that they manifest. We must spend time in prayer and in the Word of God so we can arm ourselves for battle. *"Put on the whole armour of God, that ye may be able to stand against the wiles of the devil."* (Ephesians 6:11)

Who's Gonna Tell Me
(For all of God's princesses)

Who is gonna tell me that I'm beautiful?
Who is gonna tell me it's not just outward but within?
Who is gonna tell me that I'm brave?
Who is gonna tell me that I'm nobody's slave?
That I can achieve all I set out to do . . . that I can win . . .
That I'm more than a conqueror in this world of sin?
Who is gonna fill me in?
Tell me about this world's temptations . . .
The fear and the violence in the nations . . .
And what about him?
Who is gonna warn me?
Touching me softly, whispering in my ear . . .
Being felt up only to be let down.
Who's gonna tell me he won't stay around?
Got girls around the town.
Thinking I'm in love but instead lost in lust.
Lost my trust,
total disgust 'cause love's a bust.
Who's gonna tell me it's not a fairytale?
Love is not a song on a radio.
I was feeling it tho', til the commercial break.
I'm asking you . . .
Who is gonna tell me it's a sacrifice
and not a one way street?
Love includes pain.
Love doesn't always feel good,

but is so worth the gain.
Love is 1 Corinthians 13.
Who is gonna tell me love is He?
The Creator, the Maker, the Giver and Taker of all things.
Who is gonna show me love, show me Him?
Who is gonna teach me the Word?
Who is gonna shine light my way?
Who is gonna help me see it's worth living another day?
Because this world is only showing me hate.
The falseness, the fakeness, the fear, the filthy and the foul.
I need redemption now.
I need a hope to hold onto.
I need a Savior to come to my rescue.
Who is gonna tell me He's the only One to make me whole?
JESUS,
Who is gonna tell me?

A Conversation

I must admit, you got me good.
Never thought you would.
You didn't seem like the deceiving type.
Your words felt so good.
Thought your lips were spitting truth,
but truthfully you were just spitting . . .
Spitting on my heart . . .
Spitting on my trust . . .
Spitting on my time.
I'm now feeling love's a bust.
Wishing I never let you in.
Maybe my mental state wouldn't feel so shaken.
Thought I was giving my heart away,
but instead, I feel like it was taken.
I'm tired of the fakin'!

God, why can't people just be real?
Wish for a moment they could feel what I feel.
Maybe they would change.
Why does being honest have to be so strange?
So hard?
That's why I stay to myself.
Wanna put my heart on a shelf,
but I know that's not why you created it.
Others say I shouldn't be so nice and giving.
But I don't know any other way of living.

So help me to be wise.
Help me to be aware . . .
Of no good intentions and those that don't care.
'Cause I'm tired of getting walked on
like the rug of a bear.
I just want to love without fear.

Chapter 6
Defeating the Fear

Remember when you were a kid and you were afraid of the dark. You just knew the boogeyman was in your closet or there was a monster under your bed. We had an attic at my grandma's house so we also had the fear of the moth lady known as Henrietta. Now that I have children of my own, I find myself trying to convince them that there is no such thing. They were fine until they saw a popular kid's movie that had the boogeyman in it. I tried to explain to them that neither he nor monsters exist. However, they still have that fear. They want to keep the closet door closed. They still want the night light on to help dispel some of the darkness. It is hard to convince them that what they imaged in their minds is not real.

It is amazing how one person or thing can put a thought in your head that will change your whole way of thinking. That one movie has created a thought that they cannot get out of their heads. It is the same with us as adults. Now, of course we are not quick to believe in the boogeyman, but we are quick to believe the negativity that people speak to us. The phrases like, "you're going to have a hard time starting your own business," "you don't have time to go back to school," "what makes you think that God wants to use you?" These types of phrases put doubt in our minds, which then leads to the fear of failure. This is when we begin to question our abilities and goals. This is when we go back to that childhood state of mind and keep the door closed on our own dreams and prosperity. This is when we keep our eyes focused on the night lights in our life. We say we are content where we are in our lives. Sometimes we even settle to be and achieve much less than our potential, all the while neglecting the light, knowledge and wisdom that God has already placed in us. He is our Father telling us, *"Fear thou not, for I am with thee: be not dismayed; for I am thy God . . ."* (Isaiah 41:10) He has placed that talent, gift, or dream in your life for a reason. It is not to be hidden in the dark. Let it be shared with the world so that it can help somebody else. Think about it . . . you are putting off starting a business that could help someone else obtain a job. Maybe God is leading you to go back to school in order to encourage someone else who may be considering the same.

You never know how God will use you, but just know that He *does* want to use you. Learn to dispel the darkness of fear with the light that God has placed inside of you. The world is waiting. *"For God hath not given us the spirit of fear; but of power, and of love and of a sound mind."* (2 Timothy 1:7)

Ignite

There's a ticking in my spirit,
spiritual dynamite waiting to explode.
The match has been struck,
just waiting to connect to the power.
But there's a wind blowing, trying to put it out.
There's rain falling, trying to wash it out.
My soul says move it,
but my flesh won't do it.
And as the wind blows and the rain falls,
there's a war going on.
And it's hard to tell who's winning,
'cause like Paul the more I want to do right,
the more I keep on sinning.
Got the devil grinning, but not for long because . . .
There's something over the flame.
There's something giving it flare.
Could it be the power of prayer?
Could it be God's hand of mercy,
even when the devil tries to curse me?
Could it be the shadow of the most High?
He looks after the sparrow, so why not I?
Not giving up on me when I gave up on myself.
Lying on the battlefield, wounded and near defeat . . .
He picks me up, heals my scars, and plants me on my feet.
Then He whispers, "Child, the battle is already won."
So I put on my armor, hold my head high,
and on through the battle I press.

Now walking in the Spirit and no longer in the flesh,
while the flame sparks the wick
and the power of the Holy Ghost spontaneously explodes.

Facing the Storm

I was content with my position,
there in the eye of the storm.
All around me danger roared.
All around me destruction poured.
All around me lives were disassembled.
All around me the strong were made feeble.
I looked up and the sky was bright.
Sunrays beaming down on my head,
and I realized that could be me instead.
So I was grateful, I was relieved.
I was safe in the eye of the storm, comfortable in my position.
But as I looked closer,
as I neared the danger zone I dreaded so,
I began to feel weak, unsettled, and ashamed.
Although danger was there, some were being saved.
Though destruction was profound, many were rebuilt.
Though lives were disassembled, many were repaired,
and the strong were merely, made humble.
That's when it hit me . . .
If I am to grow true . . . I must go through.

Chapter 7
Just a Time of Thanks

Have you ever had a day where it seemed everybody wanted something from you? You plan to take a day for yourself to just take time and do some things you want to do, even if it is to just relax. Then before your day has really started, several people have called or text you asking for favors or errands to run. You know as soon as the phone rings or buzzes, that it is no one checking on you to see how you are doing or just to say hi. You know that it is someone wanting or needing a favor. If you are like me and have a heart of compassion, you find it hard to say no, even if it does cut into the plans that you have already made. It seems like someone always wants or needs something from you.

Can you imagine what it would be like if God had a cellphone? Or even a call center? I imagine that the phone lines would stay busy. I can only imagine how many of those phone calls are request. Now imagine this . . . God had two call centers; one for request and one for gratitude. Which call center do you think would be the busiest? I am sure the request hotline would be the busiest. We are so quick to plead and ask God for things and changes in our lives. Yet how often do we just say, "Lord, I am talking to You just because I want to thank You." Yet, He listens to each one of them. He does not complain because He loves us. Now, He may not grant every single request, but He grants us more than we deserve.

When I get home my children love to run, grab and hug on me as I come in the door. Often times their greeting goes, "MOMMY!!!! Can you . . .?" Now, they are 5 and 7, and I understand that they are still learning how to greet and show interest in a person's needs and well-being. So, I am teaching them not to just say hello and make request, but to also show the person that they care about them by asking how their day was. I am teaching them not to only be concerned about their desires, but to take into consideration the needs of others and having common courtesy. They are getting better, but when they forget, my response is, "Hi Jeremiah and Silas!!! Mommy's day was great! Thank you for asking!" They shamefully put their heads down as they remember that they need to show care and concern then they greet me again the right way.

I am reminded of how we treat God this way sometimes. We can get up and go all day without acknowledging and thanking Him for all of the love and grace He provides us, but as soon as we have a desire or need, we are quick to make our request known. God just wants us to love and worship Him in return. He wants us to show more gratitude and appreciation for who He is. This is the essence of our creation. Yet, we often allow the cares of this life to overshadow and cloud our thoughts and focus, which should be Him and His will for our lives.

Try this . . . as you go through your day make two list. The first will be of request you make to God throughout the day. This includes the mumbling under your breath, "Lord, get me through this day . . . ," every request. The second list will be of all the things that you have thanked God for throughout the day. This includes the mumblings of, "Thank God . . . ," every form of thanks. At the end of the day, if the request list is longer than the thanks list, then you may want to start getting on the gratitude hotline more often. Take time throughout the day to just say thank You Lord, even for the little things. He would love to hear it! *"Enter*

into His gates with thanksgiving, and into His courts with praise: be thankful unto Him, and bless His name."
(Psalms 100:4)

Thank You Lord For the Breeze
(For Mama)

When the money is low and the chips are down,
    (Thank You Lord for the breeze)
You give me a song that erases my frown.
    (Thank You Lord for the breeze)
When my family is gone and no friends are nigh,
    (Thank You Lord for the breeze)
You put joy in my heart that makes me laugh instead of cry.
    (Thank You Lord for the breeze)
When I throw up my hands wanting to leave things undone,
    (Thank You Lord for the breeze)
You help me to lift up my head and see how far I've come.
So, thank You Lord . . . for the breeze.

Epiphany

To know that You trust us with life is overwhelming!
What have we done to deserve such a gift?
Life . . . how extraordinary!
It can be compared to nothing.
Life is like . . .
life is . . .
that's just it . . .
life just is!
You are Beginning and End,
when there was nothing in the earth,
You created life.
When life became contaminated,
You purified it with water.
When sin corrupted life,
You sent Your Son to restore it.
And when all is said and done,
and our Christian race is won,
You will again give life . . .
Even more abundantly.
Thank You for life!

Order Information

To contact Leah Nicole for
Speaking engagements or book orders
please send email to:

LNWB80@gmail.com

You may also order paperback books from Amazon.com.

www.ingramcontent.com/pod-product-compliance
Lightning Source LLC
Chambersburg PA
CBHW050606300426
44112CB00013B/2101